I See You Sincerely

Krista Tibbs

ISBN: 978-0-9818803-8-9

Friction Publishing Paperback English Edition
Printed in the United States of America
10 9 8 7 6 5 4 3 2 1

Ω FRICTION

This book is for you.

The person who
gave you this book
wants to say:

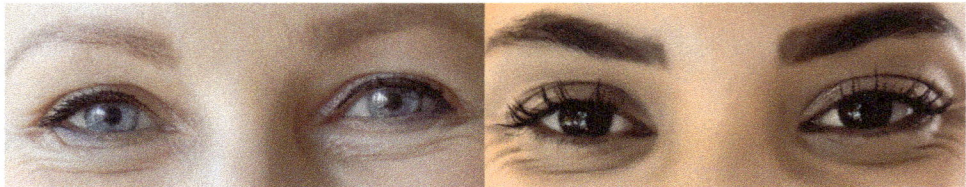

I see you. I care about you.
You are important. You are loved.

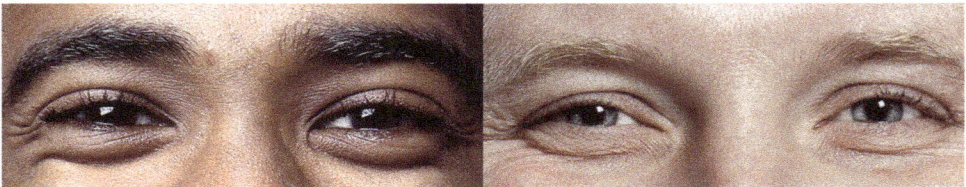

It might be hard to believe sometimes.

Maybe you feel alone.

Maybe you doubt that people in your life even know what true love looks like.

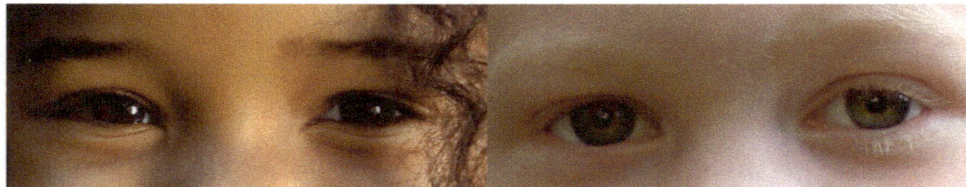

I'll show you. I'll be there.
You are valuable. You are loved.

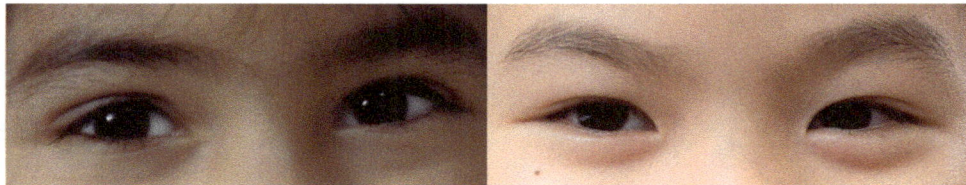

When you hurt and cry and ask why,

so do I.

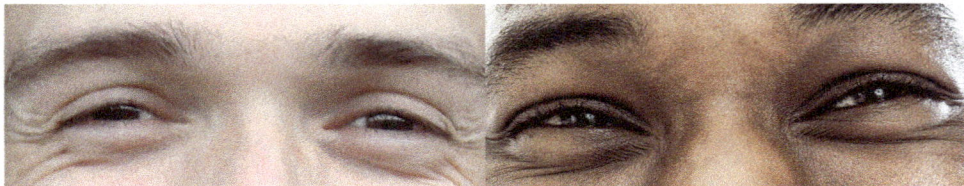

I know you. I am with you.
You have a purpose. You are loved.

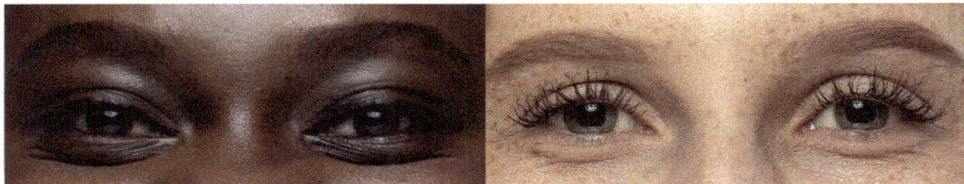

Broken people
can do awful things
in this broken world.

But whatever
has been done to you
or whatever
you have done....

I'll lend you strength so you can face it.

You are forgiven. You are loved.

Deep in your soul you are still

whole and good and mine.

Search with all your heart

and you will find me.

I want you.
I love you.
You matter.

Sincerely,
God

Image Attributions